Marilyn Monroe

A celebration of the most iconic woman
from Hollywood's golden era

Parragon

Bath • New York • Cologne • Melbourne • Delhi
Hong Kong • Shenzhen • Singapore • Amsterdam

This edition published by Parragon Books Ltd in 2014
and distributed by

Parragon Inc.
440 Park Avenue South, 13th Floor
New York, NY 10016
www.parragon.com

Creative concept by The Picture Desk
All photographs from The Kobal Collection
Written by Gabrielle Mander
Designed by Beth Kalynka
Project managed by Frances Prior-Reeves
Production by Joe Xavier

ISBN 978-1-4723-5135-7

Printed in China

Introduction

Who was Marilyn Monroe? Audiences knew her as a gloriously beautiful, vulnerable, blonde bombshell, at once innocent and alluring, who appeared on the silver screen in comedies like *Gentlemen Prefer Blondes* and *Some Like it Hot*, and dramas like *Niagara* and *River of No Return*, all of which showcased her amazing figure and curiously seductive voice. The cliché—"Men wanted her and women wanted to be her"—was coined for Marilyn.

Goddess or diva?

But directors, actors, husbands, and the studio executives knew an insecure, pill-popping diva, who kept everyone waiting on set—a goddess, with feet of clay. Perhaps the dichotomy lies in her fabled metamorphosis. Marilyn Monroe, actress and chanteuse, wanted to be taken seriously, but fantasist Norma Jeane Mortenson, born on June 1, 1926 in Los Angeles, California, just wanted to escape into a world where she would be loved and recognized—the movies.

Teen dreams

Norma Jeane's childhood was a tragedy. Her mother was committed to a mental hospital, and the tiny child was shuffled between "Aunt Grace," foster homes, and the orphanage. A poor kid whom nobody loved enough to keep. She was exploited and overlooked and feared that she too would go insane. But as her figure blossomed in adolescence, she realized that she could and did attract attention; she had "something," and other people could see it too.

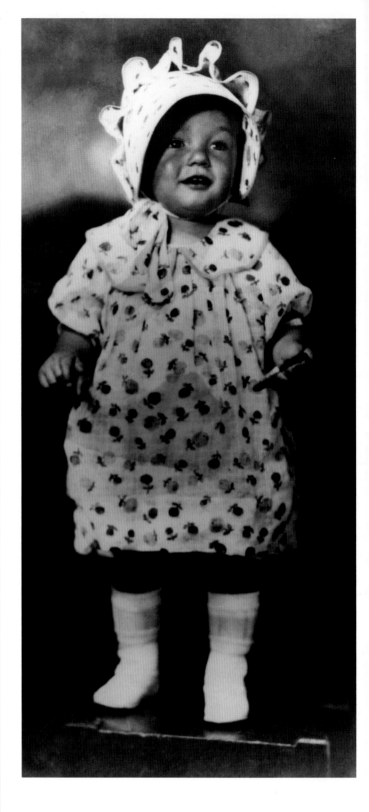

Above: A charming portrait of little Norma Jeane, age about two years and evidently dressed in her best for the photo. Norma Jeane already exhibits Marilyn's charm.

Opposite: Marilyn had a gift for combining allure with a sense of fun.

Norma Jeane somehow survived her dysfunctional, unstable, and disruptive childhood. In 1942, in an attempt to avoid another foster home, the sixteen-year-old married reluctant, sometime boyfriend, Jim Dougherty, in an arrangement suggested by her then foster parents. Norma Jeane was not unhappy: at least she was no longer an orphan and she had a home of her own. Patriotic Jim enlisted in the Merchant Marine in 1943, and Norma Jeane worked in the Radioplane Munitions Factory and became a model with the Blue Book Modeling Agency. The Doughertys divorced amicably in 1946.

Goodbye, Norma Jeane

It was 20th Century Fox that "discovered" the newly blonde Norma Jeane, and suggested the name "Marilyn" to her. She chose "Monroe" herself; it was her mother's maiden name, and she believed that she was descended from President Monroe. Marilyn left sad Norma Jeane behind. Marilyn was indefinably and undeniably beautiful, and with every penny going toward drama lessons, she could sing and dance and play both comedy and drama. Although her looks and refreshing sexuality continually distracted everyone from her talent, she was an actress and people would love her—at last!

Top: The wedding of Norma Jeane Mortenson to Jim Dougherty.

Bottom: Marilyn Monroe emerged to "walk on" in several pictures like *Dangerous Years* for 20th Century Fox, and this bit part in *Scudda Hoo! Scudda Hay!*

Opposite: By 1948, Columbia had picked up Marilyn's contract, and she had her first major role in *Ladies of the Chorus*.

By 1949, Marilyn had met agent Johnny Hyde of the William Morris Agency, who secured her a part in the movie that effectively launched her career—*The Asphalt Jungle* (1950). In 1951, 20th Century Fox upgraded her regular six-month contracts to one lasting seven years, and in the first half of the fifties, Marilyn graduated from slight comedies to the movies that made her famous. In 1954, she married baseball star Joe DiMaggio, although they divorced in the same year.

She created her own studio in 1955 with Milton Greene—Marilyn Monroe Productions—exacerbating ongoing disagreements with Fox. She also studied with Lee Strasberg and, in 1956, cerebral playwright Arthur Miller became her third husband. Sadly, this marriage did not last, and Marilyn's dependence on prescription drugs deepened.

The final curtain

Much has been written about Marilyn's relationship with the Kennedys, which some believe contributed to her lonely death by overdose in August 1962, but in truth it remains a mystery. Did she take her own life or was her ending like her beginning—a tragic series of events? All too briefly, Marilyn Monroe lit up motion pictures and established herself forever as an enchanting icon.

Opposite: This snapshot of Marilyn in 1949 offers a glimpse of the potential 20th Century Fox saw in her.

Right: Frank Powolny took this seductive portrait of Marilyn for 20th Century Fox in 1953.

All about Marilyn

Opposite: This beautiful, seductive image of the young star, by Frank Powolny, was taken in 1950. Marilyn's modeling experience was invaluable.

Top: Monroe invented the classic pinup pose of the 1950s: shoulders forward, smile with lips apart, and a direct gaze to camera. Once again, Frank Powolny was responsible for the pose in this now iconic look.

Bottom: MGM portrait photographer Eric Carpenter photographed a more sophisticated siren in a publicity still for *The Asphalt Jungle* (1950).

Dangerous Years

Postwar U.S.A. was terrified of the new generation of young people—"teenagers." These youngsters had money in their pockets and rebellion in their hearts, or so their parents thought. *Dangerous Years* (1947) is one of a number of movies made at the time, which played to moms' and dads' worst fears.

Teenage kicks

Jeff Carter has cleaned up town by providing wholesome entertainment for the young in the form of a boys' club. But young hoodlum Danny Jones (Billy Halop) has other ideas. He encourages "the gang," Doris (Ann E. Todd), Willy (Scotty Beckett), and Leo (Darryl Hickman), to hang out at the Gopher Hole, the dive where Evie (Marilyn Monroe) works as a waitress.

Right: Evie, the waitress at the Gopher Hole, with Jeff Carter in Arthur Pierson's 1947 movie. Marilyn's walk-on part was one of many that she was pleased to get in the earliest days of her Hollywood career. She had six-month contracts with both Columbia and 20th Century Fox, but there were dozens of starlets looking for a break into the big time.

Scudda Hoo! Scudda Hay!

Scudda Hoo! Scudda Hay! (1948) is a rather gentle little movie, perhaps more "B movie" than blockbuster, but good old-fashioned entertainment. It is a simple story of country folk. A farmhand, with a crush on the farmer's daughter, buys two mules from the farmer to add to his assets and subsequent allure. He is the only one who can handle this recalcitrant pair. His brother is a rival for the farmer's fair daughter's affections. Jolly japes ensue, but will true love triumph in the end?

The cutting-room floor

Marilyn was very excited about this movie. For one thing she had a line to say, "Hello," and that line was to one of the stars of the movie, June Haver. Then she had a bit in a canoe. Things were looking up. Sadly, Marilyn's one-line part never made it to the final cut, but she was slowly making her way and, as a contract player, she expected further opportunities.

Left: Marilyn, the much fabled "girl in canoe" from *Scudda Hoo! Scudda Hay!* directed by F. Hugh Herbert for 20th Century Fox. Marilyn enjoyed a platonic friendship with one of the studio heads around this time—Mr. Joe Schenck. They had met at one of the many parties that Marilyn attended for the free food and in the hope of being noticed. This friendship did not prevent her from later being dropped by the studio president, Darryl F. Zanuck.

Ladies
of the
Chorus

In her first real part, in *Ladies of the Chorus* (1948), Marilyn had an opportunity to showcase the versatility of her acting, as well as the talents for which she had first been noticed. Peggy Martin (Marilyn Monroe) and her mother, former burlesque star Mae (Adele Jergens), are employed in the chorus line. In a classic tale of the theater, when Bubbles, the featured dancer, leaves the show, Peggy has the chance to go out a chorus girl and come back a star.

Love in the limelight

Fame is not enough for young Peggy and she falls in love with Randy Carroll (Rand Brooks), a wealthy young man with a disapproving mother. Mae fears that Peggy will be hurt, as their love will never be enough to bridge the social gap between the pair. Marilyn is luminous in this part and she really shows that her acting, singing, and dancing classes had not been wasted. Inevitably, her figure attracts great attention.

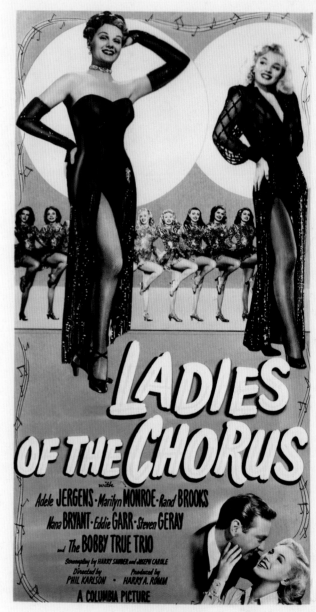

Top: Mae and Peggy prepare for Peggy's great opportunity.

Bottom: In this poster for the movie, Marilyn gets her first proper billing in *Ladies of the Chorus*, directed by Phil Karlson.

Opposite: Center stage at last, Peggy stands out from the crowd.

Love Happy

In the life of a starlet in Hollywood in 1949, any part was a good part, and Marilyn heard about this one while networking at a lunch counter. She discovered that United Artists were looking for a girl to do some retakes in *Love Happy* (1949), starring Groucho, Chico, and Harpo Marx and directed by David Miller.

Something fishy?

The movie is a typical Marx Brothers caper, involving young Broadway hopefuls living on pilfered food provided by Harpo and unknowingly concealing a sardine can in which are hidden the Romanoff diamonds. Marilyn has a walk-on part as a client of Detective Sam Grunion (Groucho Marx). Harpo and Groucho auditioned Marilyn themselves, and Marilyn said that Groucho, having met her, added in a line so that it would be a speaking part. The line was, Marilyn: "Some men are following me." Groucho: "Really? I can't understand why."

Below: Groucho and Marilyn on the set of *Love Happy*. On meeting Marilyn, Groucho is quoted as saying, "It's Mae West, Theda Bara, and Bo Peep all rolled into one; we shoot the scene tomorrow morning. Come early." Louella Parsons mentioned Marilyn in her influential column after this, saying that the producer Lester Cowan was about to offer her a contract. Marilyn was ecstatic. It never came, but she did do a tour to promote the movie.

A Ticket to Tomahawk

A Ticket to Tomahawk (1950) directed by Richard Sale, features an all-star cast, including Anne Baxter, Dan Dailey, Rory Calhoun, and Walter Brennan, with Marilyn Monroe as Clara. Marilyn had the chance to showcase her dancing and singing as part of the ensemble.

include a troupe of dancing girls, including Clara, and there may be an opportunity for a song or two to speed them on their way.

Race against time

It is 1876 and there is fierce competition between the stagecoach line and the new steam locomotive company. Kit must get the train to town in time and persuades Johnny to come along. The passengers

Below: Marion Marshall, Joyce Mackenzie, and Marilyn Monroe in a scene from *A Ticket to Tomahawk*.

The Asphalt Jungle

The Asphalt Jungle (1950) was nominated for four Oscars. This gritty, noir drama features a gang of criminals planning a major, foolproof jewelry store heist. "Doc" Riedenschneider (Sam Jaffe) is the brains, with Dix Handley (Sterling Hayden) and Alonzo Emmerich (Louis Calhern) to assist and fence the goods, respectively. Marilyn plays Emmerich's "niece." As with all foolproof plans, this one starts to unravel and it is every man and woman for themselves.

Great casting

It was agent Johnny Hyde who helped Marilyn to get the part in this, her breakthrough movie. Allegedly, he and Marilyn were lovers. In any event he truly had her best interests at heart, and his belief in her gave her the confidence to audition for the great John Huston, who said, "I cast her because she was so damn good."

Right: Marilyn in a little black dress. She auditioned for director John Huston lying on the floor and said that her characterization was, to paraphrase Groucho, "Mae West, Theda Bara, and Little Bo Peep—in tight, silk lounging pajamas."

Opposite: The "avuncular" Louis Calhern and his little "niece" Marilyn in a movie portrait for *The Asphalt Jungle*.

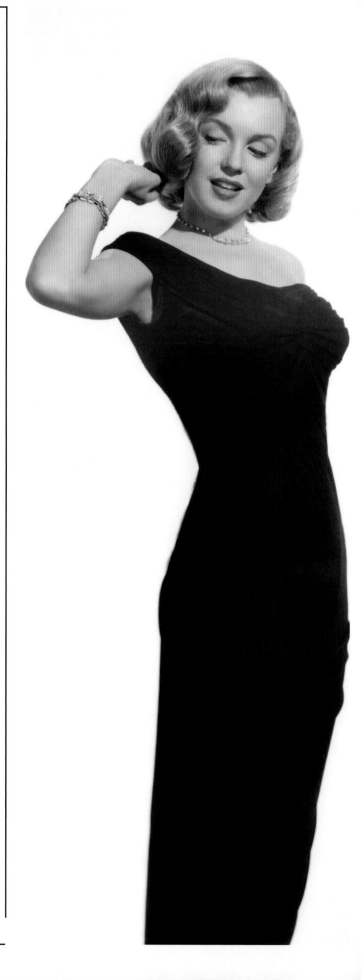

The Fireball

The Fireball (1950) is based on the almost true story of Johnny Casar (Mickey Rooney), the Catholic boy who runs away from an orphanage run by priest Father O'Hara (Pat O'Brien). Johnny knows that he can make it big as a roller skater, although he is in danger of being sidetracked by the alluring but shallow Polly (Marilyn Monroe), who is only attracted by his success in the rink, and risks losing Mary (Beverly Tyler), who truly loves him. This was a relatively small but effective part for Marilyn, undertaken as part of her short-term contract with 20th Century Fox.

Triumph and tragedy

Tragically, Johnny's hopes and dreams are threatened by the onset of polio. The early 1950s were a time of great anxiety for parents everywhere. Polio had reached near epidemic proportions in the United States and Europe and presented a particular threat to the young. Audiences were interested in this story, starring one of Hollywood's favorite former teenage actors Mickey Rooney (then aged 30) and featuring the new blonde bombshell.

Left: Marilyn Monroe, Mickey Rooney, and James Brown at the rink side. Marilyn and hundreds of other starlets were very poorly paid as bit-part players. She even had to provide her own wardrobe. She wore this dress in two other movies at this time: *All About Eve* and *Home Town Story*.

Love and Marriage

Top: Norma Jeane and her husband Jim Dougherty. Sixteen-year-old Norma Jeane married Jim in 1942, to avoid "legal orphan" status (and a return to the orphanage) when her foster parents moved out of the state. She said that they were "friends with sexual privileges." Although they were not unhappy, the couple divorced in 1946. While Jim was at sea, Marilyn took up modeling.

Bottom: Two great American heroes, Marilyn and baseball legend Joe DiMaggio, seen here in 1954. Joe was very kind to Marilyn, but quiet and introverted. Although used to press attention, he was ill-prepared for the pressure of Marilyn's popularity. He was also unhappy about Marilyn's image as a sex symbol. The couple married in January and divorced in October, but remained friends.

Opposite: In June 1956, Marilyn surprised the world when she married playwright Arthur Miller. Marilyn genuinely admired and revered her husband's intelligence and fell in love with his mind. She also hoped that Arthur's appreciation of her would show the world that she was intelligent as well as beautiful. Miller supported her attempts to be taken more seriously as an actress. Sadly, Marilyn suffered three miscarriages during their marriage. They were divorced in 1961.

All About Eve

All About Eve (1950) is universally regarded as a classic of American cinema and a triumph for its stars Bette Davis and George Sanders, winner of the Academy Award for Best Supporting Actor. Director Joseph L. Mankiewicz wrote the sparkling screenplay, for which he won one of two Oscars; the other was for Best Director. In total, *All About Eve* earned six Oscars, including Best Picture and Best Costume Design (Edith Head and Charles Le Maire).

Moving up

The plot centers on the declining career of Margo Channing (Bette Davis), a successful stage actress, and the machinations of devoted fan Eve Harrington (Anne Baxter), the young woman who becomes her assistant with the intention of replacing Margo on stage and stealing her life. In one of the few serious performances at this stage of her career, Marilyn looks absolutely beautiful and acts convincingly, albeit in the minor supporting role of Miss Casswell.

Below: Bette Davis, Marilyn Monroe, and George Sanders in a scene still from *All About Eve*. Marilyn had met Sanders years before, when she attended a Hollywood party. She recalled that the inebriated star proposed marriage within minutes of meeting her and then immediately fell asleep.

Opposite: Frank Powolny's 20th Century Fox publicity portrait of Marilyn for *All About Eve*.

Home Town Story

In *Home Town Story* (1951), Blake Washburn (Jeffrey Lynn) believes that the town's leading manufacturer is to blame for the failure of his political aspirations. He takes over his uncle's newspaper in an attempt to fight the power of big business. However, his views change when the company is instrumental in averting a tragedy.

Take a letter

Marilyn makes the most of her screen time, serving her acting apprenticeship in another minor role as a secretary. This MGM movie was good experience and certainly added to her industry profile. It is said that *Home Town Story* started life as a commercial for General Motors and the virtue of big business in general, which may account for the rather labored plot and stilted direction.

Top: Secretary Iris Martin (Marilyn Monroe) deflates the ego of reporter Slim Haskins (Alan Hale Jr.) as they exchange pleasantries, featuring the second appearance of Marilyn's own dress, as seen in *The Fireball* and *All About Eve*.

Bottom: Marilyn's role as a secretary involved a great deal of walking about, followed lingeringly by the camera, in this form-fitting knitted dress.

As Young As You Feel

The satirical comedy, *As Young As You Feel* (1951), was Marilyn's first movie under her upgraded contract with 20th Century Fox. This time she signed up for seven years. In an unlikely plot, aging printer John Hodges (Monty Woolley) attempts to resist enforced retirement, at age 65, from the ACME printing company. He conspires to undermine their plans by visiting the works in the guise of the boss of its parent company.

Screen presence

Much hilarity ensues, but this low-budget movie also carries a subtle message to traditional audiences about the erosion of the values of service and loyalty. Marilyn is beautiful and although her part is small, her screen presence is great as Harriet, the beautiful secretary (again).

Left: Horace Gallagher (Wallace Brown) and Harriet (Marilyn Monroe) in a scene still. It was during the production of this movie that Marilyn first met her future husband, Arthur Miller.

Love Nest

Love Nest (1951) is the comic tale of a New York apartment building and the antics of its inhabitants, who undermine the artistic efforts of the owner, would-be novelist Jim Scott (William Lundigan), and disturb the peace of mind of his wife Connie (June Haver). When a former WAC colleague of Jim's, Roberta "Bobbie" Stevens (Marilyn Monroe), moves in, things become even more complicated.

A cuckoo in the nest

Love Nest is an accomplished movie with outstanding performances from its star cast, and Marilyn is no exception as Bobbie, a substantial supporting role. However, her sex appeal is still exploited to the full. It was said that the bathing suit she wears in one scene was considered so risqué that director Joseph Newman ordered a closed set during shooting.

Top: Bobbie arrives, to the consternation of Connie. June Haver was a very big star at this time. She was the star of *Scudda Hay! Scudda Hoo!*, Marilyn's second movie, although then Marilyn's line didn't make the final cut.

Bottom: Marilyn looks glamorous and elegant in this 1951 costume-test picture for *Love Nest*. At least she didn't have to wear her own clothes.

Let's Make It Legal

Hugh Halsworth (Macdonald Carey) and his wife Miriam (Claudette Colbert) are counting down the hours until their divorce becomes final at midnight, in *Let's Make It Legal* (1951). Hugh is a compulsive gambler and Miriam has had enough, but he is finding it hard to leave, especially when Miriam's former beau Victor (Zachary Scott) shows up. Enter Joyce Mannering (Marilyn Monroe), who has a gold digger's interest in Victor.

Poet in rags

Marilyn seemed to be typecast in the role of beautiful, sexy, mercenary distraction in the movies that she made for 20th Century Fox at this time. Although she was gradually earning more screen time, her acting skills were only occasionally required. Arthur Miller described her as, "…a poet on a street corner trying to recite to a crowd pulling at her clothes."

Below: Hugh and Joyce, Victor and Miriam lead one another a merry dance in this scene still. Despite her supporting role, Marilyn was fortunate to act with veteran stars Colbert, Carey, and Scott.

Clash by Night

Legendary director Fritz Lang directed this RKO gem, *Clash by Night* (1952), and got a terrific performance from Marilyn Monroe (Peggy), costarring with Barbara Stanwyck as cynical, world-weary Mae Doyle. Mae returns to her hometown, a fishing village, and moves in with her brother Joe (Keith Andes). Although she settles for marriage and motherhood with Jerry D'Amato (Paul Douglas), she begins an affair with Jerry's sinister friend Earl (Robert Ryan). Joe's sweetheart Peggy works in the cannery and Joe fears that she will become like Mae and spoil their love.

An "A movie"

Marilyn could be more than proud to have worked on this movie with such a distinguished cast. Clifford Odets wrote the play on which the screenplay was based and the dialogue is as superb as the direction, camerawork, and performances.

Top: Joe and Peggy in a scene still from *Clash by Night*. Marilyn looks stunning and acts beautifully in this movie. Her mother had worked at RKO as an editor during Marilyn's early childhood, and the studio was the source of Marilyn's dream of becoming an actress.

Bottom: Peggy may be becoming as restless as Mae in this scene. Will life with Joe be enough for her?

We're Not Married!

We're Not Married! (1952) tells five stories of couples who discover that, although each has lived together as husband and wife for some time, the judge who performed the ceremony was not yet licensed to marry them. Each couple has issues with his or her spouse at this point in their marriage, which the news may exacerbate or improve.

Miss Mississippi

Annabel Norris (Marilyn Monroe) has just won Mrs. Mississippi and is in the running for Mrs. America, much to the consternation of her husband Jeff (David Wayne). This news disqualifies her, but she promptly enters Miss Mississippi and wins, naturally. This light comedy from 20th Century Fox and director Edmund Goulding played to what the studio saw as Marilyn's strengths.

Right: It's win-win for Annabel, married or not, though Jeff may not agree in this scene from *We're Not Married!*

Don't Bother to Knock

You've never met her type before...

...a wicked sensation as the lonely girl in Room 809!

RICHARD **WIDMARK**
MARILYN **MONROE**
in
Don't Bother to Knock

20th CENTURY-FOX

NOT SUITABLE FOR CHILDREN

WITH ANNE BANCROFT · DONNA CORCORAN · JEANNE CAGNEY · LURENE TUTTLE · ELISHA COOK, Jr. · JIM BACKUS · VERNA FELTON

PRODUCED BY JULIAN BLAUSTEIN · DIRECTED BY ROY BAKER · SCREEN PLAY BY DANIEL TARADASH

Marilyn Monroe and Richard Widmark, playing Nell Forbes and Jed Towers, star in this 1952 psychological thriller, *Don't Bother to Knock*. Airline pilot Jed has split up with his girlfriend, singer Lyn Lesley (Anne Bancroft), and finds himself at a loose end in the hotel where she works. Spotting the gorgeous Nell at her window, he invites himself to her room for a drink. However, Nell is not all she seems and gradually Jed realizes that she has severe problems and may be a danger to the child asleep in the next room.

Success at last

Marilyn is really, truly superb in this movie and categorically proves that she can act in serious parts. She remains incredibly beautiful, but she also draws upon her own experience of her mother's disintegration into madness to inform her performance, with spectacular success.

Left: The graphics for this poster advertising the movie give equal billing to Widmark and Monroe, although the illustration doesn't do justice to the seriousness of Marilyn's role as Nell.

Opposite: Nell's faraway look should signal a warning to Jed in this scene from *Don't Bother to Knock*, directed by Roy Ward Baker. Jed is too dazzled by her looks and his luck to heed the signs.

Full House

Full House is an anthology of five stories by O. Henry, set in New York between 1902 and 1910. Marilyn plays a streetwalker and was fortunate enough to costar with Charles Laughton, as Soapy, in "The Cop and the Anthem" (1952), the most critically acclaimed of the five stories. Soapy is a hobo who confides to fellow bum Horace that he is going to get arrested so he can spend the winter in a warm jail cell.

The wrong girl

The movie follows his various attempts to achieve this lofty aim. All are unsuccessful, especially the scheme in which he plans to get caught accosting a virtuous woman. The cop is more interested in arresting her for soliciting, as she turns out to be the unnamed streetwalker (Marilyn). The other stories are "The Clarion Call," "The Last Leaf," "The Ransom of Red Chief," and "The Gift of the Magi." Henry Koster directed "The Cop and the Anthem." The directorial credits for the rest of the anthology read like a list of 1950s cinema luminaries: Henry Hathaway, Jean Negulesco, Howard Hawkes, and Henry King.

Right: Soapy attempts to accost the streetwalker, and both seem surprised by the result of this encounter.

Inset: Marilyn as the streetwalker tries to convince the cop that she did not accost Soapy.

Monkey Business

Monkey Business (1952) is a "screwball comedy" directed by Howard Hawks, starring Cary Grant as scientist Dr. Barnaby Fulton, Ginger Rogers as his wife Edwina, Charles Coburn as his boss Oliver Oxley, and Marilyn Monroe as Oxley's secretary Lois Laurel. But the real star is the chimp that mixes and adds a youth serum to the watercooler, causing Barnaby's and Edwina's behavior to regress to childhood. Confusion and mayhem ensue.

Man and boy

Marilyn the smoldering secretary gives a very good performance as a foil to Cary Grant's preoccupied scientist, impervious to her charms as well as to his drug-induced alter ego, the naughty schoolboy. She also feels the wrath of Edwina in the form of a catapult, when Edwina reverts to being an uninhibited tomboy. It's all jolly good fun, if vaguely reminiscent of Howard Hawks's *Bringing up Baby*, also starring Grant.

Top: Marilyn and Cary Grant look as if they are really enjoying roller skating as they share Dr. Fulton's second childhood.

Bottom: Once again Marilyn has equal billing in an all-star cast on this poster for the movie. Even though her part was peripheral at best, 20th Century Fox were not ashamed to cash in on her sex appeal and her popularity with the public.

Opposite: Lois attempts to interest Dr. Fulton. Marilyn's typing speed should have been phenomenal by 1952, considering the number of times she played a glamorous secretary.

Niagara

Rose Loomis (Marilyn Monroe) is young, beautiful, passionate, and restless. Her husband George (Joseph Cotten) is an older, depressed, jealous ex-serviceman. The location is a honeymoon hotel at Niagara Falls, and passions are running high. Rose makes no attempt to disguise her interest in other men, and George is right to suspect that she is having an affair. But Rose has more than stolen passion in mind.

Twisted dreams

If director Henry Hathaway had made *Niagara* (1953) in black and white, its cinematography, plot twists, and narrative would classify it as film noir. In Technicolor, it is a great thriller with spectacular scenery, including Marilyn's staggeringly seductive dress. This is the first bona fide starring role for Marilyn, and she sings too.

Inset: Marilyn kept the dress that she wore to such great effect in *Niagara*. Finally, here she had the opportunity to prove that she was a great actress. Rose is incredibly sexy, of course, but Marilyn never appears cheap or tawdry in this or any of her movies.

Opposite: Marilyn is very much in character as the fearless femme fatale. Confident in the power of her own allure, she poses against the backdrop of the magnificent Niagara Falls.

Gentlemen Prefer Blondes

Stunning Lorelei Lee (Marilyn Monroe) and gorgeous Dorothy Shaw (Jane Russell), one blonde and one brunette, are showgirls looking for husbands. Directed by Howard Hawks, *Gentlemen Prefer Blondes* (1953) is set mainly on a transatlantic voyage to France, which may provide romantic Dorothy with a handsome husband and consolidate Lorelei's engagement to Gus Esmond Jr. (Tommy Noonan), a millionaire nerd.

Diamonds are a girl's best friend

A private detective, Ernie Malone (Elliott Reid), is employed by Mr. Esmond Sr. to catch Lorelei in some romantic indiscretion. Lorelei is fascinated by diamonds, but there is an ineffable honesty and naivety in her search for security. Malone falls for Dorothy, and Lorelei flirts innocently with Sir Francis "Piggy" Beekman (Charles Coburn), although she is most attracted to Lady Beekman's diamond tiara.

Opposite: Frank Powolny took this now famous studio portrait of the fabulous Monroe and Russell. Marilyn Monroe not only starred in the movie, she became a huge star, and the picture earned more than seven and a half million dollars for 20th Century Fox.

Top: The movie delivers everything that this poster promises: European travel, dancing, romance, and, above all, glamour.

Bottom: Together, Jane Russell and Marilyn Monroe in matching outfits have something for everyone. As a result of the movie's success, both actresses were invited to put their hand and footprints outside Grauman's Chinese Theatre, fulfilling a childhood dream for Norma Jeane.

In many ways, *Gentlemen Prefer Blondes* has stood the test of time. It is a smart, witty movie, based on Anita Loos' novel (1925) and the 1949 Broadway show of the same name, with a 1950s twist. Russell and Monroe are phenomenal in every song and dance; Russell even performs with the Olympic gymnastics team, and the songs, a mixture of the original show tunes by Jule Styne and Leo Robin and new material by Hoagy Carmichael and Harold Adamson, are all showstoppers.

"We all lose our charms"

All of us, that is, except Marilyn. Marilyn's comic performance as Lorelei is a perfect mix of innocence and self-awareness, and the songs and dances are performed faultlessly. This was the start of a run of successes for Marilyn that would establish her as a Hollywood icon.

Opposite: Lorelei finds herself trapped in the detective's cabin while she searches for incriminating pictures. The audience anticipates that the porthole presents her with a challenging escape route.

Right: "I don't want to marry him for his money; I want to marry him for *your* money. Don't you know that a man being rich is like a girl being pretty? You wouldn't marry a girl for being pretty, but doesn't it help?" Lorelei explains her rationale to Esmond Sr., but it is all in the song "Diamonds are a Girl's Best Friend." Marilyn's performance in this wonderful set piece has been often imitated, but never excelled.

How to Marry a **Millionaire**

In *How to Marry a Millionaire* (1953), flaky Pola Debevoise (Marilyn Monroe), smart Schatze Page (Lauren Bacall), and feisty Loco Dempsey (Betty Grable) are New York fashion models who are tired of the men who pursue them for their beauty, most of whom are not the marrying kind. They hatch a plot to share a luxury penthouse apartment, borrowed from tax dodger Freddie Denmark (David Wayne), and combine their talents to catch three millionaire husbands.

Bad connections

Schatze has her eye on wealthy widower J. D. Hanley (William Powell), while being pursued by ostensibly poor but handsome Tom Brookman (Cameron Mitchell). Loco gets mixed up with a married, bad-tempered businessman with dishonorable intentions, but entangled with poor, yet handsome Eben (Rory Calhoun). Pola falls in with a conman masquerading as an oil tycoon, but a missed plane brings her together with the elusive Freddie Denmark.

Opposite: Marilyn Monroe, Lauren Bacall, and Betty Grable as the three models in search of wealthy husbands. Each is dressed according to her Hollywood image. Bacall is elegant and beautiful, Monroe sexy in a swimsuit, and Grable displays her legendary fabulous legs.

Bottom: In a scene still from the movie, Marilyn conveys both great allure and total innocence.

Top: Marilyn with unknown costar in this movie portrait for *How to Marry a Millionaire*. At long last, the starlet who had to supply her own wardrobe gets to wear elegant designer clothes. Costume designers Charles Le Maire and William Travilla were nominated for an Academy Award for the movie.

Marilyn could not have imagined herself costarring with Hollywood legends Bacall and Grable while she was paying her dues in seemingly endless bit parts for 20th Century Fox. Studio head Darryl F. Zanuck could never see her potential. Even as she helped make three enormously successful movies in a row for the studio, she was involved in a dispute over the salaries and career opportunities given to studio contract players. She was suspended more than once.

Beautiful fool

Monroe had definitely discovered a talent for comedy. When she asked what her motivation was for the character of Pola, director Jean Negulesco gave her a pair of spectacles. She squeezed the comedy pips out of her screen shortsightedness without ever resorting to slapstick and, despite playing another gold digger, managed to win the audiences' approval and sympathy.

Left: Dorothy Parker said, "Men seldom make passes at girls who wear glasses." Marilyn Monroe, as Pola Debevoise, is obviously the exception that proves the rule, seen here with Betty Grable as Loco Dempsey. Both actresses gave superb performances.

River of No Return

Otto Preminger directed the drama *River of No Return* (1954), starring Marilyn Monroe as former saloon girl Kay Weston, and Robert Mitchum as farmer Matt Calder. Calder and his young son Mark (Tommy Rettig) help Kay and her gambler husband Harry (Rory Calhoun) when they lose control of their raft. Harry runs out on Kay, taking Matt's horse and rifle, leaving Matt, Mark, and Kay defenseless in the face of an imminent Indian attack.

No way back

Matt, Mark, and Kay must embark on a perilous journey downriver, from which they may never return. Recently released from prison, Matt barely knows his son, but the three must develop strong bonds to battle both hostile natives and nature. Although Marilyn was later dismissive of the movie, the screen chemistry between the stars was electric.

Opposite: The dress that Marilyn wears here as saloon girl Kay Weston contrasts with the folksy outfits she must don to brave the rapids of Canada's Athabasca River. Director Otto Preminger insisted that the stars performed their own stunts, and Marilyn was famously injured when the raft overturned.

Bottom: The poster for *River of No Return* implies that Matt and Kay fight one another as fiercely as they fight the elemental forces of nature. The inset of Kay as singer does not do justice to her performance singing the theme tune; she is mesmerizing on screen.

Top: Marilyn manages to look equally sensational in blue jeans and a camisole and in the elaborate costume she wears for her musical solo.

There's No Business Like Show Business

In 1954, Marilyn accepted an all-singing and dancing part as Vicky Parker in Irving Berlin's story of the death of vaudeville, *There's No Business Like Show Business.* Vicky is instrumental in the breakup of a tightly knit family act, the Donahues: Terence and Molly and their two sons and a daughter. Vicky steals the heart of son Tim (Donald O'Connor). In truth, Steve (Johnnie Ray) has already found a vocation as a priest, and daughter Katy (Mitzi Gaynor) wants to get married, but when Tim falls for Vicky it is the final straw.

Let's go on with the show

Troopers Molly and Terence (Ethel Merman and Dan Dailey) are the last to know of their children's defection. Marilyn's part showcased her singing and dancing, especially in the spectacular number "Heat Wave," but hers was a relatively small part, in a cast with Hollywood legends Merman and Dailey. Marilyn's costume for "Heat Wave" caused some consternation. It could reveal and suggest but she was not allowed to show her navel.

Opposite: Marilyn's costume for the number "After You Get What You Want" revealed as much as it concealed. She was still in contract negotiation with 20th Century Fox, following her rebellion and suspensions in 1953, and accepted the part to gain leverage.

Left: Marilyn and Donald O'Connor pose, in costume, for a studio portrait to promote the movie.

The Seven Year Itch

Marilyn's character in the famous Billy Wilder comedy, *The Seven Year Itch* (1955), is known only as "The Girl" who represents the notion that after seven years of faithful marriage any husband will be tempted to stray when the opportunity and a beautiful girl present themselves. Richard Sherman (Tom Ewell) is left alone in his apartment while his wife and family go out of town to escape the heat of a New York summer.

When the cat's away

He decides to take the opportunity to lead the life of a bachelor in their absence, eating and drinking whatever he feels like. He entertains the possibility of having an affair with the gorgeous but flaky blonde who lives upstairs, and who is looking for an air-conditioned haven away from the heat of her apartment.

Right: Sam Shaw took this studio shot recreating the famous scene from *The Seven Year Itch* in which, to her delight, The Girl's skirt is blown up as she stands over a subway grille on a New York street, on a sultry summer night. William Travilla designed the dress specially. It is said that it was this scene and the onlookers' reaction during the original location shooting that was the final straw for Marilyn's husband Joe DiMaggio. The couple divorced in October 1954.

Opposite: The Girl seems charmingly oblivious to Richard's attempts to get close to her at the piano and the consequences that find them on the floor.

Nothing actually happens between Richard Sherman and The Girl in *The Seven Year Itch*. The idea of adultery is all in his imagination and she is unaware of his lustful thoughts. Wilder's casting for this plot is perfect since, as Marilyn said, "People had the habit of looking at me as if I were some kind of a mirror instead of a person. They didn't see me, they saw their own lewd thoughts, then they white-masked themselves by calling me the lewd one."

Innocent fun

The tagline, "It TICKLES and TANTALIZES!—The funniest comedy since laughter began!" may have been a slight exaggeration, but *The Seven Year Itch* is very amusing. Marilyn reprises her role as the innocent seductress beautifully, and her comic timing in the delivery of her lines is impeccable. Tom Ewell won a Golden Globe for his part and Marilyn was nominated for a BAFTA.

Left: Tom Ewell and Marilyn Monroe in a studio portrait for the movie. The sofa was the height of chic in 1954.

Bus Stop

Beauregard "Bo" Decker (Don Murray) is a brash, twenty-one-year-old virgin farmer, taking the bus from Montana to a rodeo in Phoenix, Arizona, with Virgil Blessing (Arthur O'Connell), his older friend and mentor. Bo is looking for "an angel" to marry and take back to Montana. Cherie (Marilyn Monroe) is singing (badly) as a barroom hostess, playing to drunken leering men and working her way to Hollywood and her dream of becoming a movie star.

Rope 'em and Brand 'em

Bo falls in love with Cherie and ropes her like a steer, forcing her onto the bus and into an engagement. Bo must learn respect and humility before he can win Cherie, who must face both her past and her future. An enforced stopover at the eponymous bus stop provides the backdrop. Joshua Logan, who directed *Bus Stop* (1956), was an exponent of method acting, which Marilyn had been studying with Lee Strasberg, and her accomplished performance is both tremendously moving and very funny.

Opposite: Cherie is facing both her past and her future in the bus-stop diner. She had plotted her wayward course to Hollywood on the map, but is now considering abandoning her dream to go with "Bo" and fulfill his.

Top: In what is arguably her finest performance, method actor Marilyn called upon the parallels in her own life to develop the role of Cherie, a poor, lost girl dreaming of making it in male-dominated Hollywood.

Bottom: A movie portrait of Marilyn for *Bus Stop*. She mastered a Southern drawl for the part of Cherie. Frustrated at 20th Century Fox, she had formed Marilyn Monroe Productions in 1955, then she married Arthur Miller in June 1956.

The Prince and the Showgirl

Laurence Olivier produced, directed, and starred in *The Prince and the Showgirl* (1957), written by Terence Rattigan, which was made in conjunction with Marilyn Monroe Productions. Marilyn costarred as Edwardian London showgirl Elsie Marina. Olivier plays Charles, the Prince Regent of a politically pivotal, fictional European country, "Carpathia," who is a guest in London in 1911 for the coronation of George V. Prince Charles takes a fancy to Elsie Marina after seeing her performance in *The Coconut Girl*, and the British government encourages her to accept his dubious invitation to supper, promising her protection from any unwanted advances. But lovely Elsie Marina is more than equal to the situation.

Method and madness

Olivier was frustrated by Marilyn's lateness on set, her inability to remember her lines, and her search for "motivation." He was not a fan of method acting. Marilyn was intimidated and humiliated by Olivier and insecure in her relationship with Arthur Miller. Fearing mental breakdown, she became increasingly dependent on prescription drugs. It was not a happy production.

Right: The acclaimed fashion photographer Richard Avedon took this photograph of Marilyn to promote *The Prince and the Showgirl*. Young model Norma Jeane could never have dreamed that she would one day be a successful actress, posing for Avedon. The Blue Book Modeling Agency had fired the young model for having "too much sex appeal for fashion modeling."

Inset: The dream team—beauty and brains? Marilyn is pictured here with costar and director Laurence Olivier and her husband, playwright Arthur Miller.

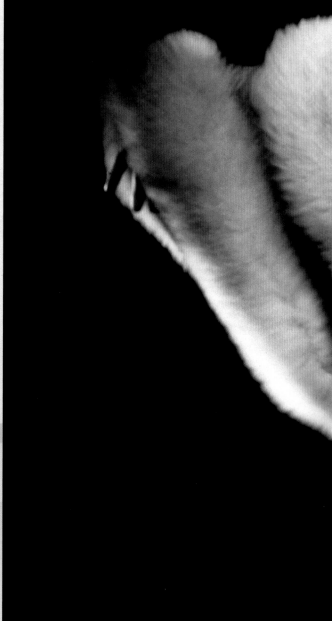

Swimwear

Top: Marilyn drew upon her experience as a pinup model for this studio portrait in 1951. She manages to make a simple black one-piece look sexy and glamorous. Perhaps it is the ankle-strapped high heels.

Bottom: This Bert Reisfeld photograph from 1953 shows Marilyn in another swimsuit, this time with a jewel accessory. Perhaps the subtext is that Marilyn is so hot that she sets off firecrackers with her explosive good looks.

Opposite: This Bert Reisfeld image from 1953 is reminiscent of the glamour magazines of the late 1940s. Marilyn posed for these when she left the munitions factory. The model had to maintain a pose like this for hours while illustrations were drawn from life. They were usually coy, seductive poses with props, like this one.

Some Like it Hot

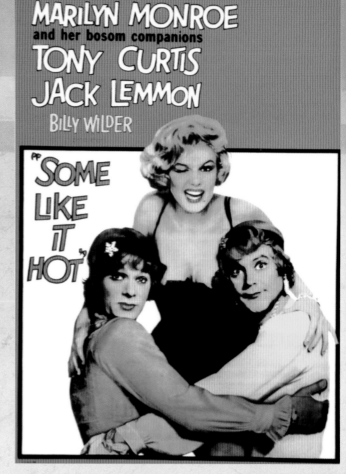

In 1958, Marilyn returned to Hollywood to make *Some Like it Hot* (1959) with legendary director Billy Wilder. Brilliantly, he cast Marilyn as the ditzy, ukulele-playing, blonde bombshell, Sugar Kane Kowalczyk, singer with an all-girl jazz band. Booked to play in Miami, the band provides the perfect hiding place for Joe and Jerry (Tony Curtis and Jack Lemmon), two musicians who have witnessed the St. Valentine's Day Massacre in Chicago, perpetrated by gangster "Spats" Colombo (George Raft).

Boys will be boys

However, they have to play the parts of Josephine and Daphne to get the gig, and they must maintain their disguises and resist the considerable charms of Sugar Kane, close up and personal, for the duration.

Top: The graphics for this poster show Tony Curtis and Jack Lemmon as their female alter egos—Marilyn's "bosom companions."

Bottom: Marilyn tempts Tony Curtis, who claims to be impotent in his second role as a phony oil millionaire.

Opposite: Marilyn sings on the final night of Sweet Sue's band's engagement in Miami. Critics commented that Marilyn was even more curvaceous than usual in this movie. In fact, she was pregnant at the time, and the early symptoms contributed to her unreliability on set. Sadly, she suffered a miscarriage, the first of three in eighteen months.

United Artists' *Some Like it Hot* was nominated for six Academy Awards, winning one for Best Costume Design. It is probably Marilyn's most popular and famous movie for modern audiences. This was her third movie with director Billy Wilder, who always tried to make the production easy for her, filming the Miami scenes in California, for example, to avoid too much travel for her.

Black and white

It was her husband, Arthur Miller, who persuaded Marilyn to take the part. Wilder said, "Sugar Kane was the weakest part in the picture, so we solved that with the strongest possible casting." Marilyn was disappointed that Wilder was to shoot the movie in black and white. He was convinced that Curtis and Lemmon's female impersonation would not be convincing if he shot in color.

Opposite: Marilyn Monroe, Tony Curtis (standing), and Jack Lemmon (top right). Josephine and Daphne share a sleeping berth with the girls in the band, on the overnight train to Miami. Both Joe and Jerry are stunned by Sugar's charms. On set the actors, especially Curtis, were frustrated by Marilyn's now legendary lateness and the number of takes involved in each scene.

Left: Marilyn is incandescent on screen, reprising her trademark combination of naivety and apparently unconscious, overwhelming sex appeal.

Tony Curtis plays a third part in the movie, when he disguises himself as an impotent millionaire to try to win Sugar. One of the high points of his impersonation for the audience at the time was his adoption of Cary Grant's clipped accent for the part. He later denied that he had said that kissing Marilyn was like kissing Hitler.

"Well, nobody's perfect"

Despite the tensions between the stars, the performances and direction are faultless, and none of the difficulties show in the final cut. The picture stands the test of time, even today, and its famous final line has been a movie quiz winner for half a century.

Opposite: The boys gain insight into the female mind as Sugar explains to a spellbound "Daphne" and "Josephine" why she has sworn off trumpet players for ever. This is discouraging news for "Josephine."

Below: Girl talk with Sugar Kane; Jack Lemmon and Marilyn both won Golden Globes for this picture.

Let's Make Love

Marilyn owed 20th Century Fox a movie, and they picked *Let's Make Love* (1960) directed by George Cukor. Billionaire Jean-Marc Clement (Yves Montand) discovers that he is to be satirized in an off-Broadway revue. In an attempt to get the inside story, he visits rehearsals and is mistaken for the actor playing him in the show. He is anxious to get closer to the beautiful leading lady, Amanda Dell (Marilyn Monroe), so continues the deception.

Sex, lies, and celluloid

The character of Clement is said to have been based on reclusive millionaire Howard Hughes, and Marilyn fought to have Montand cast in the role when Gregory Peck dropped out. In spite of strong set musical numbers, like "My Heart Belongs to Daddy," the presence of Tony Randall as Coffman, and an alleged affair between Marilyn and Montand, the movie lacks heart.

Opposite: A scene still from a dance sequence in *Let's Make Love*, in 1960. Despite unbilled cameos from Milton Berle, Bing Crosby, and Gene Kelly, and the presence of English 1950s pop singer Frankie Vaughan, the movie was a "turkey." Marilyn said Amanda Dell was "The worst part I ever had."

Right: Marilyn in a wistful mood in this between-takes shot during filming. Marilyn admired costar Yves Montand. The script calls for her to fall in love with him, and Montand told the press that he and Marilyn were lovers. Still married to Arthur Miller, she was furious.

The Misfits

The Misfits (1961), directed by John Huston, is the story of beautiful, recently divorced Roslyn Tabor (Marilyn Monroe), who finds herself entangled with aging cowboy Gay Langland (Clark Gable) and his friends Guido (Eli Wallach) and Perce (Montgomery Clift) in Reno, Nevada. When Roslyn's friend Isabelle Steers (Thelma Ritter) joins them, the group embarks on an adventure that challenges their experiences of the past and their hopes and dreams of future happiness.

Manly pursuits

The men accept a commission to round up wild mustangs, destined for the slaughterhouse, which threatens the growing relationship between Gay and sensitive Roslyn. Can the pair overcome their fears and differences to create a new family together?

Opposite: A movie portrait of Clark Gable and Marilyn Monroe. At last Marilyn was starring with the man she had fantasized about as a role model for her unknown father during her lonely childhood.

Left: Off set during filming, appearances are deceptive. Marilyn looks relaxed and happy, but the shooting was very demanding in punishing heat, and she had become very dependent on prescription drugs and pills.

The Misfits started auspiciously with Marilyn's reunion with director John Huston, who had been responsible for her first big break in *The Asphalt Jungle*. The screenplay was written by her husband, Arthur Miller, with a tailor-made starring role for her, and her costar was her hero, Clark Gable. However, the filming was unbelievably taxing. Huston was drinking heavily and Marilyn struggled with the many changes that Miller made to the script on set and was continually late and forgetful. Her dependence on drugs deepened.

Soft focus

Huston stopped production while Marilyn went into detox and shot her close-ups in soft focus when she returned, but the death knell had sounded for Marilyn's marriage to Miller. In retrospect, critics agreed that both Gable and Monroe gave outstanding performances, but the movie was not a box-office success. Most significantly, it turned out to be Clark Gable's last screen appearance. A fortnight after filming ended, he died of a heart attack.

Right: Montgomery Clift, Marilyn Monroe, and Clark Gable have remained luminous stars of the great days of Hollywood. The lives of all three were defined by tragedy.

Opposite: Arthur Miller supported Marilyn's ambition to be taken seriously as an actress. He believed in her ability but was challenged by her insecurity. In this photograph, Marilyn's unhappiness and the strain of the production is evident in her face.

Something's Got to Give

Something's Got to Give (1962) was to be a remake of *My Favorite Wife* in which Ellen Arden (Monroe) is declared dead some years after her disappearance at sea, and her husband Nick (Dean Martin) remarries. However, Ellen is not dead and returns to the family home to reclaim her husband and two children. George Cukor was all set to direct a funny, touching comedy. Sadly, after only 37 minutes of film, Marilyn was fired by Fox. The film was never finished, although the footage still exists, including the famous nude bathing scene.

Below: Marilyn looks a little thin but still incandescently beautiful in this, one of the few stills from the footage of her last movie.

The End

Marilyn was ready for the next stage of her life. She renegotiated a much more advantageous contract with the studio, giving her more artistic control and a better salary, but before she could begin work, she died tragically of an overdose of sleeping pills in 1962. Despite many conspiracy theories, it seems infinitely possible that her death was a tragic accident, rather than suicide. As in life, people seem quite prepared to believe the worst of the beautiful star. Perhaps a "white trash" girl who was not ashamed of her allure, but worked hard to become an accomplished actress, dancer, and singer would never be given the benefit of the doubt. But thankfully, lovely Marilyn became, and remains, a glorious, global icon of the 20th century, loved by men and women alike.

Filmography

The Shocking Miss Pilgrim (1947) (voice)

Dangerous Years (1947)

Scudda Hoo! Scudda Hay! (1948)

Green Grass of Wyoming (1948)

Ladies of the Chorus (1948)

Love Happy (1949)

A Ticket to Tomahawk (1950)

The Asphalt Jungle (1950)

Right Cross (1950)

The Fireball (1950)

All About Eve (1950)

Home Town Story (1951)

As Young as You Feel (1951)

Love Nest (1951)

Let's Make It Legal (1951)

Clash by Night (1952)

We're Not Married! (1952)

Don't Bother to Knock (1952)

Full House (1952)

Monkey Business (1952)

Niagara (1953)

Gentlemen Prefer Blondes (1953)

How to Marry a Millionaire (1953)

There's No Business Like Show Business (1954)

River of No Return (1954)

The Seven Year Itch (1955)

Bus Stop (1956)

The Prince and the Showgirl (1957)

Some Like It Hot (1959)

Let's Make Love (1960)

The Misfits (1961)

Something's Got to Give (1962)

Golden Globes, U.S.A.

1962	Won	Henrietta Award
		World Film Favorite—Female
1960	Won	Golden Globe Best Motion Picture Actress—
		Musical/Comedy
		Some Like It Hot (1959)
1957	Nominated	Golden Globe Best Motion Picture Actress—
		Comedy/Musical
		Bus Stop (1956)
1954	Won	Henrietta Award
		World Film Favorite—Female

BAFTA Awards, U.K.

1958	Nominated	BAFTA Film Award—Best Foreign Actress
		The Prince and the Showgirl (1957)
1956	Nominated	BAFTA Film Award—Best Foreign Actress
		The Seven Year Itch (1955) U.S.A.

Images from

THE KOBAL COLLECTION

The Kobal Collection owes its existence to the vision, courage, talent, and energy of the men and women who created the movie industry and whose legacies live on through the movies they made, the studios they built, and the publicity photographs they took. Kobal collects, preserves, organizes, and makes these images available to enhance our understanding and enjoyment of this cinematic art.

Thank you to all of the photographers (known and unknown) and the movie distribution and production companies whose images appear in this book. We apologize in advance for any omissions or neglect, and will be pleased to make any corrections in future editions.

3 20th Century Fox/Gene Kornman, 4–5 20th Century Fox, 6 Columbia, 7 20th Century Fox, 8–10T 20th Century Fox/Frank Powolny, 10B MGM/Eric Carpenter, 12–15 20th Century Fox, 16–17 Columbia, 18 United Artists, 19 20th Century Fox, 20–21 MGM, 22 20th Century Fox, 26–27 20th Century Fox, 28 MGM, 29–31 20th Century Fox, 32 RKO, 33–42 20th Century Fox, 43 Frank Powolny/20th Century Fox, 44–53 20th Century Fox, 54–57 Sam Shaw/Shaw Family Archives/20th Century Fox, 58–59 20th Century Fox, 61 Richard Avedon/Warner Bros, 62–63B Bert Reisfeld/20th Century Fox, 63T MGM, 64–69 United Artists, 70–71 20th Century Fox, 72–75 United Artists/7 Arts, 76–77 20th Century Fox

Front cover image: 20th Century Fox/Frank Powolny